A POSITIVE *Spirit*

Uplifting the Mind & Enriching the Soul

Sheila Edwards

Trilogy Christian Publishers

A Wholly Owned Subsidiary of Trinity Broadcasting Network
2442 Michelle Drive
Tustin, CA 92780

10 9 8 7 6 5 4 3 2 1
Library of Congress Cataloging-in-Publication Data is available.
ISBN 978-1-64088-547-9 (Print Book)
ISBN 978-1-64088-548-6 (ebook)

Dedication

Josiah Glen Edwards

This book is dedicated to my beloved son, Josiah Glen Edwards, who taught me to love and be loved unconditionally. His love for God ignited my desire to discover my divine purpose. I'm blessed by his tenacity, perseverance, and positive spirit radiating through his life. His diligence, encouragement, and faith birthed A Positive Spirit LLC.

My Mom

My mom, Elizabeth Bernice Godfrey, taught me to live victoriously through God's love, mercy, and grace. She lived by example, teaching me to put God first and everything else would fall into place. Her love and faith bring so much peace and joy through life's journey.

My Brother, Glen Godfrey

Thank you for being my biggest supporter and speaking words of wisdom to my heart throughout the years. I am so proud of your accomplishments and all that God has done in your life! Our lives are forever intertwined through God's love and grace. May God continue to bless you, today and always.

Friends and Family

Friends and family are priceless jewels. They are God's special gifts to make our world a little brighter. Giving thanks, my friends and family, for your love, encouragement, and support throughout every season of my life. I pray God will continue to grant favor, peace, love, and mercy in your lives.

Acknowledgement

Ms. Wanda
The host of "Full Circle" on Sacramento's number one community radio station, 97.5 FM KDEE. May God continue to bless SpeakHER Consulting. Your vision and insight as a public speaker, coach, consultant, motivational speaker, and trainer have blessed my heart. Thank you for keeping me accountable for the vision! I appreciate your time, insight, and dedication.

Introduction

When we respond to life's challenges with a positive spirit, we open the door to our divine destiny.

A Positive Spirit is an inspirational book with a Christian perspective. It gives God's plan for uplifting the mind and enriching the soul. When we respond to life's challenges with a positive spirit, we open the door to our divine destiny.

God is faithful throughout life's journey, opening the right doors and closing the wrong ones. Life happens in seasons, and we learn and grow through transformational change. Each step is hand-crafted by God, effortlessly working with our future in mind. When we put God first in our lives with a positive spirit, He opens the door to our divine destiny.

"God is our refuge and strength, a very present help in trouble."
(Psalm 46:1, KJV)

Table of Contents

CHAPTER 1

Peace Comes from God

***When we live in our purpose, there is satisfaction of the soul,
destiny is revealed, and the world is blessed.***

ELEVATE YOUR PERSPECTIVE

A positive spirit means allowing God to elevate your perspective. Life's challenges open our mind, heart, soul, and spirit to God's divine plan for our lives. When our goals and motives align with our purpose, we win!

> *"I can do all things through Christ which strengtheneth me."*
> *(Philippians 4:13, KJV)*

A LITTLE PEACE

The peace of God surpasses all understanding, transcending natural sight. When we trust God by faith, our lives open to His divine plan. He knows the desires of our hearts, our silent prayer requests, our deepest thoughts and emotions. Bring every burden, trial, and discomforting situation to Him in prayer. God strengthens, empowers, encourages, and guides us through life's journey.

> *"And the peace of God, which passeth all understanding,*
> *shall keep your hearts and minds through Christ Jesus."*
> *(Philippians 4:7, KJV)*

CHANGE

God walks beside us in situations of inevitable change. He whispers wisdom in our ears and directs us along life's journey. Change is easier when we realize God has a divine plan for our lives.

> *"And we know that all things work together for good to them that love God,*
> *to them who are the called according to his purpose."*
> *(Romans 8:28, KJV)*

God is working with your future in mind.

PRAYER

God sees the tears you hide, the sleepless nights, and the concern for your family. He is a loving Father, concerned about His children. Whatever your need is today, God is working with your future in mind. There is no load too heavy, burden too troublesome, or situation too tough for God to handle. Whatever your need is today, give it to God in prayer.

> *"Cast thy burden upon the Lord, and he shall sustain thee."*
> *(Psalm 55:22, KJV)*

JOY

Joy is not predicated on one's circumstances. It's knowing God is always in control. Despite what we see, how we feel, and what's going on around us, God will never fail us in our time of need. He is there, gently reaching out with love, mercy, and grace. God's love is open to all who will receive; He's just one simple prayer away.

> *"For God so loved the world, that he gave his only begotten Son, that whosoever believeth in him should not perish, but have everlasting life."*
> *(John 3:16, KJV)*

It's a New Day!

THIS IS YOUR SEASON

Everything happens for a reason, sometimes only for a season, to grow us into God's divine plan and purpose for our lives. Each circumstance, obstacle, blessing, and promise bring us closer to our destiny. We can be confident knowing God is there, loving, encouraging, and giving us peace; the world can't satisfy.

> *"To everything there is a season,*
> *and a time to every purpose under the heaven."*
> *(Ecclesiastes 3:1, KJV)*

BE SET FREE

Do you want joy? Do you want peace? Do you long for freedom beyond comprehension? This comes from God. In Him there is freedom, liberty, growth, understanding, joy, grace, mercy, and unconditional love. Without God, we would be limited by our own abilities. His direction brings clarity, His guidance brings peace, His lead brings purpose, and His presence brings security.

> *"Stand fast therefore in the liberty wherewith Christ hath made us free."*
> *(Galatians 5:1, KJV)*

A NEW DAY

We all have a gift, an encouraging word, a unique talent, a strength, a divine calling in our lives. Explore and be who God created you to be. There are new and exciting days ahead, and God is waiting with loving arms to guide us through anything. He loves us, adores us, and is there for us through life's journey.

> *"This is the day which the Lord hath made;*
> *we will rejoice and be glad in it."*
> *(Psalm 118:24, KJV)*

Action Items:
1. Write down three goals that will bring peace in your life.
2. Name three unique, beautiful things about yourself.
3. Write down three things you are grateful for and thank God for them.

CHAPTER 2

Open Your Mind to Possibilities

Your past is a catalyst for great things to come.

GREAT THINGS AHEAD

Your past is a catalyst for great things ahead. You are a blessing to others because of your experiences. Your testimony has the power to change lives! Look forward to the future with expectancy and great anticipation! God has a divine plan for your life that exceeds your expectations. Have faith, press forward, and receive God's blessings in your life.

> *"My soul, wait thou only upon God; for my expectation is from him."*
> *(Psalm 62:5, KJV)*

OBSTACLES INTO BLESSINGS

God can turn our obstacles into blessings. Each situation creates a growth experience. When we share the beauty of lessons learned, we propel ourselves to the next level in God. Nothing in life happens by accident. There is a reason, a season for everything. We can trust God through the stormy seasons, because He has the divine power to bring us out victoriously.

> *"And let us not be weary in well-doing:*
> *for in due season we shall reap, if we faint not."*
> *(Galatians 6:9, KJV)*

WE ARE NOT ALONE

God is there to help us through life's challenges, waiting to hear our concerns and helping us through life's journey. We are not alone today. There are many who walked in similar shoes, trusted God despite hindering circumstances, and came out victoriously. Our situations will become testimonies of walking by faith.

> *"For we walk by faith, not by sight."*
> *(2 Corinthians 5:7, KJV)*

POSSIBILITIES

If you could see yourself through God's eyes, the beauty, strength, faith, diligence, and perseverance would overwhelm you. Your past does not define your future in God. Tap into your dreams and realize the possibilities. This is your time to receive God's blessings in your life.

> *"I will instruct thee and teach thee in the way which thou shalt go:*
> *I will guide thee with mine eye."*
> *(Psalm 32:8, KJV)*

Past lessons are a gift to your future.

THIS IS IT

It's time to move forward with your heart's desire by not allowing your past to paralyze your future. Look to the future with hope, grace, and love, knowing your best days are ahead. Brace yourself to receive God's best for you and your beautiful family. It's your time for a new beginning of purpose and destiny.

> *"But seek ye first the kingdom of God, and his righteousness;*
> *and all these things shall be added unto you."*
> *(Matthew 6:33, KJV)*

THERE IS TRIUMPH AHEAD

Regret not the past, but learn from the transformational growth of your experience. Challenging experiences transcend us to a level of strength and great testimonies of faith, mercy, and perseverance. Look to the future with hope, triumph, and the ability to see past your circumstances. There is joy, peace, love, and mercy ahead.

> *"Now the God of hope fill you with all joy and peace in believing,*
> *that ye may abound in hope."*
> *(Romans 15:13, KJV)*

TAKE A CHANCE

Don't let fear sabotage your destiny. Listen to the whisper of hope in your ears; feel God's love and support resting delicately on your shoulders. As a father cares for his children, God cares for every aspect of your life. Move forward, knowing you can succeed far beyond your imagination.

"For God hath not given us the spirit of fear; but of power,
and of love, and of a sound mind."
(2 Timothy 1:7, KJV)

TIME TO BE HEALED

It's time to be free, healed, and full of God's best for your life. Each day, experience, situation, and obstacle are growth opportunities to a new dimension in God. The journey is sometimes hard, the road is bumpy, the heart is broken, but the result leads to a testimony that will help others.

Things don't happen by accident; they are stepping-stones on your journey to your purpose. Don't lose hope or give up in the valley of despair; the best is yet to come.

"All things are possible to him that believeth."
(Mark 9:23, KJV)

A BRIGHTER PERSPECTIVE

Every day is an opportunity to seize God's best for your life. Your future is not predicated on your past. Choose to give the world a brighter perspective through your life. You are marvelous and have the power to be a positive influence in someone's life.

"Therefore if any man be in Christ, he is a new creature:
old things are passed away; behold, all things are become new."
(2 Corinthians 5:17, KJV)

WHAT A DIFFERENCE A DAY MAKES

Each day is full of wonderful possibilities when we allow God to whisper His message of love, peace, hope, and joy into our hearts. He lifts our burdens, cares, concerns, and insecurities. There is no problem too difficult, burden too heavy, or person too broken for Him. God's grace uplifts the mind and enriches the soul through a positive spirit.

"Casting all your care upon him; for he careth for you."
(1 Peter 5:7, KJV)

A NEW SEASON

The sky is the limit to what can be achieved through your life. It's time to claim the abundant and bountiful blessings God has prepared for you. Let go of the past and embrace your future with the peace of God.

If you are holding on to past hurts, trust issues, uncertainties, doubts, and other negative feelings, you are blocking future blessings. Give yourself the gift of forgiveness and move forward in a new direction, unlocking the beauty inside and living your purpose.

Divine assignments change the world by delivering the unique gift only you can offer the world. Reach beyond your comfort zone and receive what God has for you! There is abundant life and freedom in God.

"I can do all things through Christ which strengtheneth me."
(Philippians 4:13, KJV)

MOVE FORWARD

There is a purpose, season, and time for everything. Life is full of growth experiences, transitioning us to our purpose and destiny. Choose to move forward through adversity with grace and deliverance.

"For with God nothing shall be impossible."
(Luke 1:37, KJV)

Adversity transforms into growth opportunities.

MAKE IT COUNT

What's going on in your life right now is not by accident. Part of our life's journey is growing through adversity. Our experiences propel growth beyond our imagination. Make a conscious effort to move forward in strength, courage, and faith, ready for the challenge ahead.

The time is now; no more looking back and making excuses. Grab your vision and start living it. Take the first step and make the leap! Your divine destiny is only a few steps away.

Put your trials and tribulations into perspective by growing in wisdom.

Overcome your obstacles, embrace your vision, and move forward. No one else can be who God created you to be.

"Fear thou not; for I am with thee: be not dismayed; for I am thy God: I will strengthen thee; yea, I will help thee; yea, I will uphold thee with the right hand of my righteousness."
(Isaiah 41:10, KJV)

LOOKING AHEAD

It's hard to focus on the future through the lens of the past. Persevere with courage by forgiving past failures, mistakes, and disappointments, and move forward with great expectation.

Be authentic and follow your heart; discover the road to your purpose and destiny. Unlock the door to God's promises and blessings for your life. Adversity transforms into growth opportunities, giving strength to move forward in faith towards our purpose and divine destiny.

"And we know that all things work together for good to them that love God, to them who are the called according to his purpose."
(Romans 8:28, KJV)

Action Items:
1. Write down three goals you've been avoiding.
2. Set time daily to pursue your goal.
3. Write the potential results of accomplishing your goal.

CHAPTER 3

of

Share Your Story

Today's journey is tomorrow's testimony.

MENTORS

Mentorship is an opportunity to sow into the lives of others by uplifting, guiding, teaching, and creating a bond transcending the test of time. When we share our expertise, wisdom, knowledge, and experience, others become men and women of honor, courage, faith, and hope. Mentors are priceless treasures sowing gifts of leadership, character, integrity, legacy, wisdom, and hope into the next generation.

"For the Lord giveth wisdom:
out of his mouth cometh knowledge and understanding."
(Proverbs 2:6, KJV)

BE A VESSEL OF CHANGE

Change allows us to reach beyond the boundaries of the norm into a new dimension, a new horizon. Be a vessel of transformational change by allowing God to shine through your life, choices, dreams, and interactions.

Be a blessing to others though your experiences with kindness, grace, and love. Inspire others to be positive with mercy, grace, charity, humanity, empathy, and forgiveness.

"Let your light so shine before men, that they may see your good works,
and glorify your Father which is in heaven."
(Matthew 5:16, KJV)

MAKE A DIFFERENCE

Life's challenges place us in a position to help others along life's journey. We go through tough things—seemingly unbearable—that allow us to grow, learn, and become catalysts for transformational change. Our collective experiences give strength and support to others.

"We then that are strong ought to bear the infirmities of the weak."
(Romans 15:1, KJV)

TODAY'S JOURNEY

Today's journey is tomorrow's testimony. Everything in life is not always personal. Things happen for us to grow to another level where we can bless others through our experiences. Your trials and tribulations are not in vain. Keep trusting God, and He will bring you out victoriously!

"And they overcame him by the blood of the Lamb,
and by the word of their testimony."
(Revelation 12:11, KJV)

GRATEFUL

God is amazingly faithful in our lives. Trials and tribulations become our transition to our divine destiny when we allow faith to transform worry into faith. God has a unique plan for everyone. Life's journey is a stepping-stone to living testimonies of God's love, grace, and provision. Through life's journey, God places special people in our lives to make the road a little sweeter.

I thank God for a tremendous group of family and friends who have prayed for and supported me throughout life's journey. My prayer is that families remain grounded in faith, knowing God does not make mistakes. We can place our trust in Him, knowing He will always direct us to the right path with love, mercy, and grace.

"O give thanks unto the LORD; for he is good:
because his mercy endureth forever."
(Psalm 118:1, KJV)

Life is a challenging journey, but lessons learned transcend you
to a level where your testimony can change a person's life.

EACH DAY IS A NEW OPPORTUNITY

Each day is an opportunity to learn from past experiences and grow into the divine place God has uniquely created just for you. His plan leads you to a place where your trials become a transformational testimony of divine faith.

"A man's heart deviseth his way: but the Lord directeth his steps."
(Proverbs 16:9, KJV)

SHOW LOVE BY GIVING TIME

Reach out and touch someone's soul by giving your time to one in need. Moments spent helping others are like beautiful flowers, resting in heaven's garden. Using priceless time to help others unlocks the door to God's heart, and His light shines through your life. Do not hesitate; you have a divine invitation to shine. Let your life be a mirror that reflects God's image to the world.

"Look not every man on his own things,
but every man also on the things of others."
(Philippians 2:4, KJV)

There is triumph and joy on the other side of your obstacles.

GOD KNOWS HOW TO GET YOUR ATTENTION

Have you ever found yourself getting closer to God after adversity and opposition? God wants to be first in our lives—part of our decisions, efforts, pursuits, and goals.

The reward of learning from life's experiences is the jewel buried deep in times of trouble. The jewel is the testimony of triumph and transformational change. God is always bigger than our situation; we can trust He's holding our hand with unconditional love.

Growth is learning from our mistakes and soaring to the next level in God. He teaches through life experiences and challenges us to overcome victoriously. Look for the jewel in your circumstances. What is God trying to teach you? What is the jewel you must learn and share with others? Be of good courage; there is triumph and joy on the other side of your obstacles!

"For we walk by faith, not by sight."
(2 Corinthians 5:7, KJV)

God is always working behind the scenes with your future in mind.

SPEAK THE TRUTH

When we speak the truth of our pain, experiences, and challenging situations, we become transparent in uplifting the hearts and minds of others.

The 3-step Challenge:
1. Will you share your story to help others?
2. Will you speak the truth and bring light to the world?
3. Will you be transparent in uplifting the hearts and minds of others with a positive spirit?

"Wherefore comfort yourselves together, and edify one another,
even as also ye do."
(1 Thessalonians 5:11, KJV)

Action Items:
1. Look for the jewel in your circumstances.
2. What is God trying to tell you?
3. How can your experience uplift others?

CHAPTER 4

Inspire Others

**You are a beautiful being, full of life and
wonderful talent to offer the world.**

REACH OUT

There are those whose shoulders we stood on when we thought we were at
the end of our journey, those who sowed into our lives and encouraged us to
succeed despite hindering circumstances, those who prayed and sought God
when we would have given up. We did not get where we are today alone.
Let's return the favor by giving thanks, reaching out, and blessing someone
else.

"Give, and it shall be given unto you;
good measure, pressed down, and shaken together, and running over,
shall men give into your bosom."
(Luke 6:38, KJV)

YOU ARE AWESOME

Your special way of inspiring others brings life to dying situations, and your
words of encouragement are evident in your positive spirit. Don't take your
gifts and talents for granted; you are awesome and special just the way God
created you!

"Every good gift and every perfect gift is from above."
(James 1:17, KJV)

YOU ARE BEAUTIFUL

You are a beautiful being, full of life and wonderful talent to offer the
world. Don't be afraid to share your expertise with others. Everyone is born
with a special gift, something that makes them unique and full of life. Take
a moment to discover what makes your heart sing and commit to it. Your
diligence can make a positive difference in someone's life.

"Delight thyself also in the Lord:
and he shall give thee the desires of thine heart."
(Psalm 37:4, KJV)

GRATEFUL

Challenging times make us stronger, wiser, and more beautiful than before.
Life's journey is full of obstacles and amazing experiences. Stand tall
and be grateful for the wonderful person God has created you to be. He is
faithful and is always working behind the scenes with your future in mind.

"God is faithful."
(1 Corinthians 1:9, KJV)

UPLIFTING OTHERS

We are peacemakers, trailblazers, and legends in the making. When we
uplift others, we build a legacy of joy, peace and honor. As we share our
stories, strengths, and weaknesses, we become a blueprint for helping others
persevere through life's challenges. When we speak our truth, freedom is
released, and we are set free!

"If the Son therefore shall make you free, ye shall be free indeed."
(John 8:36, KJV)

RESTORATION

All the experiences, hurt, pain, and events leading to today are not by
accident. Move towards your future with hope, determination, and
perseverance. Be a living testimony of what God can do through the
restoration process.

"He will be with thee, he will not fail thee, neither forsake thee."
(Deuteronomy 31:8, KJV)

MOVING FORWARD

There is so much goodness, grace, and love ahead of you. Look to the future
with great anticipation. Move forward, knowing you're not alone with God
on your side. He's beside you, holding your hand, guiding you forward to
the next step of excellence in your life.

"Show me thy ways, O Lord; teach me thy paths."
(Psalm 25:4, KJV)

YOUR TIME IS NOW

Today is your day of peace, joy, and restoration. I pray God's deliverance for those suffering from broken hearts, chronic illness, pain, and feeling overwhelmed by life's journey. God is here to heal the frustrated, the misunderstood, the forgotten, and those silently contemplating giving up. God has not forgotten you.

"If thou canst believe, all things are possible to him that believeth."
(Mark 9:23, KJV)

If you could see your life through God's eyes, you would be amazed.

EVERY DAY

God has a divine plan for your life. The situation plaguing your life is a stepping-stone to great days ahead. You are going to bless many people with your testimony of triumph through adversity. God is preparing you for a place where the world will look at you and see Him.

Your story is one of perseverance and faith. You are destined for greatness and uniquely constructed to be a blessing to others through your life. Don't give up! If you could see your future through God's eyes, you would be overwhelmed. Every day is an opportunity for a new beginning.

"Now thanks be unto God, which always causeth us to triumph in Christ."
(2 Corinthians 2:14, KJV)

GOD HAS SO MUCH FOR YOU

Learn the beauty of lessons learned through adversity; the growth process changes lives through a positive spirit. If you could see your future through God's eyes, you would be amazed. Listen as God whispers His message of hope and love to your heart. Do not be overwhelmed by the sound of your pain, knowing God has a solution for every problem.

"But my God shall supply all your need according
to his riches in glory by Christ Jesus."
(Philippians 4:19, KJV)

GROWTH

Growth challenges our comfort zone though lessons learned. Adversity challenges us see God as our answer. Overcoming opposition victoriously through faith allows the world to see God's favor in our lives. Don't be afraid of the capacity God sees in you. It's the road map to your divine destiny.

> *"Now unto him that is able to do exceeding abundantly*
> *above all that we ask or think."*
> *(Ephesians 3:20, KJV)*

FREEDOM IS INEVITABLE IN GOD

Circumstances bring anxiety, depression, and worry. Our heart longs for a place where freedom is inevitable. God's love, mercy, peace, and grace bring strength, and His power emerges out of adversity. You are innately unique, created by God in His image. Life's challenging situations cause doubt, but faith in God brings hope, knowing our future is not predicated on our circumstances.

> *"Fear thou not; for I am with thee:*
> *be not dismayed; for I am thy God:*
> *I will strengthen thee; yea, I will help thee."*
> *(Isaiah 41:10, KJV)*

Action Items:
1. Name three ways you can inspire others.
2. What have your circumstances taught you about moving forward?
3. What changes will you make to leave your comfort zone?

CHAPTER 5

5

Trust in God

Hard times produce unparalleled strength.

TRUST GOD TODAY

A single decision can change the course of your life. Whatever your need is today—healing, a restored relationship, financial freedom, deliverance from loneliness or depression—God is there for you. There is not a situation too tough, a burden too heavy, or a load too big that God cannot bear. Trust God today and bring every aspect of your life to God in prayer!

"Trust in the Lord with all thine heart;
and lean not unto thine own understanding.
In all thy ways acknowledge him, and he shall direct thy paths."
(Proverbs 3:5-6, KJV)

OVERCOME WITH GOD

When things are falling apart, God gives hope and power to overcome adversity through His mercy and grace. His light shines through our lives, giving hope; we know everything will be okay when we place our trust in His divine plan for our lives.

"God is our refuge and strength, a very present help in trouble."
(Psalm 46:1, KJV)

TRANSCEND TODAY

God brings peace, joy, and rejuvenation. Life is a challenging journey, but lessons learned result in living testimonies with the power to change lives. When life seems unfair, choose to react by placing your trust in God and believing in the promises of His Word.

"For we walk by faith, not by sight."
(2 Corinthians 5:7, KJV)

STRENGTH TO ENDURE

We grow through transformational change. Challenging situations are opportunities to depend on God for direction, love, and support. When our

efforts are exhausted, God gives us strength to endure, overcome, and grow into our divine destiny.

"But the word of the Lord endureth forever.
And this is the word which by the gospel is preached unto you."
(1 Peter 1:25, KJV)

GOD IS IN CONTROL

We are living testimonies of strength, resilience, perseverance, diligence, and faith through adversity. Overcoming opposition leads to the discovery of purpose and destiny. Be strong, knowing God is in control and has resolutions to our problems, answers to our questions, and strategies for His divine plan for our lives.

"Trust in the Lord with all thine heart; and lean not unto thine own
understanding. In all your ways acknowledge Him,
and he shall direct thy paths."
(Proverbs 3:5-6, KJV)

Life is a portal—
a gateway to lessons learned for a phenomenal future.

THERE IS A REASON

Life is a portal—a gateway to lessons learned for a phenomenal future. When we overcome adversity, strength emerges, and we enter a season of transformational change as God opens doors to restoration, rejuvenation, and forgiveness. Trust God to be the difference that transforms your life through faith with love, mercy, peace, hope, and grace.

"For I know the thoughts that I think toward you, saith the Lord,
thoughts of peace, and not of evil, to give you an expected end."
(Jeremiah 29:11, KJV)

SOMETHING NEW

This is the beginning of something new; God has a divine plan for your life. Receive all God's promises for you and your beautiful family. Adversity builds strength to endure life's journey. Hold on—you are going to make it by faith, knowing your best days are ahead!

> *"Behold, I make all things new. And he said unto me,*
> *Write: for these words are true and faithful."*
> *(Revelation 21:5, KJV)*

BLESSED

Life's challenges lead us to our purpose and God's divine plan for our lives. When we trust God, we open the door to true happiness, fulfillment, and contentment. Faith in God allows us to rise above pain, hardship, suffering, and despair, and to become living testimonies of restoration through adversity.

> *"The Lord is my rock, and my fortress, and my deliverer;*
> *my God, my strength, in whom I will trust."*
> *(Psalm 18:2, KJV)*

THE BEST IS YET TO COME

God's Word is not subject to our timetable. His Word transcends what we see, the boundaries of the present, and the uncertainty of the future. Be patient; God's great plans for your future are soon to unfold.

> *"Rejoicing in hope; patient in tribulation; continuing instant in prayer."*
> *(Romans 12:12, KJV)*

TO GOD BE THE GLORY

Each day brings new opportunities to live victoriously. God helps us through life's challenges with joy, mercy, grace, and peace, by replacing fear with faith, hope, and expectation.

We have the courage to be optimistic, because God gives us the positive spirit to endure life's challenges. He fills the emptiness we hide, bringing comfort, strength, and hope to an unkind world.

God's unconditional love, strength, hope, and peace help us find meaning, courage, and direction. He allows us to move forward, knowing our future is not predicated on our circumstances. A positive spirit helps us to live victoriously along life's journey.

"For in him we live, and move, and have our being."
(Acts 17:28, KJV)

Action Items:
1. What testimony will you share to uplift others?
2. Name three things God has done for you in the past.
3. How will trusting in God change your life?

CHAPTER 6

ⅉ

I Will Embrace My Destiny

***Each person has a unique purpose, destiny, gift, talent—
something special to offer the world.***

A UNIQUE PURPOSE

Each person has a unique purpose, destiny, gift, talent—something special to offer the world. Your existence is not an accident, your past is not a mistake, and your experiences are not in vain. It's tempting to give up before God's blessings materialize in your life, but don't give up. You are closer than ever to the fruit of your labor.

We are products of our experiences, challenges, hopes, and dreams. Lessons learned increase our confidence, rejuvenate our hearts, and link to our divine destiny. Be strong in the Lord; God is going to bring you out victoriously.

> *"Be strong in the Lord, and in the power of his might."*
> *(Ephesians 6:10, KJV)*

WALK INTO YOUR DIVINE DESTINY

It's time to walk into God's best for your life. Your circumstances, experiences, challenges, and lessons are not by accident. There is so much positivity, grace, love, joy, and peace ahead. Look forward to the future with great anticipation. Your future will be so much better than your past! The key is putting God first in your endeavors, and He will guide you to your purpose and divine destiny.

> *"But seek ye first the kingdom of God, and his righteousness;
> and all these things shall be added unto you."*
> *(Matthew 6:33, KJV)*

TODAY

God has a divine plan for your life. Everything that has transpired in your life has prepared you for today! When you feel discouraged, lonely, misunderstood, or overwhelmed, be encouraged, knowing God is holding your hand. There is nothing too hard for God. He will never put more on you than you can bear.

> *"If ye shall ask anything in my name, I will do it."*
> *(John 14:14, KJV)*

WISDOM

Wisdom doesn't have to explain itself. Sometimes it's best to keep quiet and let God work through your actions. Wisdom comes from God, perseverance, trials, tribulations, persecution, and life experience. God will never fail you; He's holding you up, strengthening and preparing you for the next step in your divine destiny.

> *"For the Lord giveth wisdom:*
> *out of his mouth cometh knowledge and understanding."*
> *(Proverbs 2:6, KJV)*

BLESSED BEYOND MEASURE

Today is the day for change. We are blessed beyond measure with tenacity and perseverance to receive what God has for us. Our lives are by divine design, custom-made for life's journey.

> *"Blessed is the man that trusteth in the Lord,*
> *and whose hope the Lord is."*
> *(Jeremiah 17:7, KJV)*

YOUR GATEWAY TO OPPORTUNITY

Challenges are merely a gateway to opportunity. Triumph, resilience, and beauty flow from survivorship. We stand unshaken, strengthened, and resilient. Be strong; your past was a stepping-stone to your divine purpose.

> *"Be strong and of a good courage, fear not, nor be afraid of them:*
> *for the Lord thy God, he it is that doth go with thee;*
> *he will not fail thee, nor forsake thee."*
> *(Deuteronomy 31:6, KJV)*

Don't let fear stop you from reaching your destiny.

PURSUE YOUR DREAMS

Take a chance and pursue your dreams. We all have a unique talent, gift, and divine purpose. We were destined to change lives by sharing the gifts God has placed in us. Remember, you have something special to offer the world. Deliver the dream that God placed in your heart.

"For I know the thoughts that I think toward you, saith the Lord, thoughts of peace, and not of evil, to give you an expected end."
(Jeremiah 29:11, KJV)

CHANGE

Change allows us to step into something new with endless possibilities—leaving the past, embracing the present, and looking to the future with great expectation. The world is waiting for your unique talent, vision, and purpose. Be tenacious and embrace your dreams. Don't let fear undermine your destiny.

"I can do all things through Christ which strengtheneth me."
(Philippians 4:13, KJV)

DIVINE ASSIGNMENT

Everyone has a unique purpose leading to their divine assignment. Don't allow fear, doubt, and past experiences to sabotage and paralyze your future. When failure and disappointments are used as learning opportunities, we grow and become open to God's divine plan for our lives.

When we align our lives through faith, God opens doors and strategically places people in our lives who are destined to move us forward. When we surrender to God's divine plan for our lives, He guides, directs, and leads us to our divine assignment.

"But they that wait upon the Lord shall renew their strength; they shall mount up with wings as eagles; they shall run, and not be weary; and they shall walk, and not faint."
(Isaiah 40:31, KJV)

YOU HAVE SO MUCH TO OFFER

God created us with everything we need to be successful. Our experiences are catalysts for future opportunities. The hurt, pain, struggle, and rough times lead to our purpose. Our challenges unveil hidden strengths, opening the door to new possibilities, launching us forward, and catapulting us to our divine destiny.

Situations are sometimes so horrendous, we can't see or feel the hand of God; but's He's there, guiding and holding our hand. Our trials and tribulations become living testimonies, inspiring others to succeed despite hindering circumstances.

"I will speak of thy testimonies also before kings, and will not be ashamed."
(Psalm 119:46, KJV)

POSITIVE LENSES

When we see life through positive lenses, we soar beyond the present and embrace our purpose. Life begins to change; unexpected things start to happen when we become exhausted from living life our own way. God begins shaking things up, opening doors, and creating opportunities from life's challenges, leading to our divine destiny.

"Behold, I have set before thee an open door, and no man can shut it."
(Revelation 3:8, KJV)

Action Items:
1. Are you living in your divine destiny?
2. What additional steps do you need to take?
3. What is holding you back from your purpose?

CHAPTER 7

$\mathcal{V}$

Victorious Living

You are important, uniquely made, and destined to change the world.

YOU ARE AMAZINGLY STRONG

Sometimes horrible things bring us into the path of something beautiful.
The thing that didn't destroy us becomes the catalyst for transformational
change. When we respond to life's challenges with a positive spirit, we open
the door to our divine destiny.

"Finally, my brethren, be strong in the Lord,
and in the power of his might."
(Ephesians 6:10, KJV)

CHANGE THE WORLD

God changes the world through our lives. Life grants opportunities to share
what we've learned to encourage others. Our wisdom, experiences, love,
compassion, and testimonies are imperative for transformational change.
We are important, uniquely made, and destined to change the world through
our lives.

"Every good gift and every perfect gift is from above,
and cometh down from the Father."
(James 1:17, KJV)

I CAN SEE CLEARLY NOW

The clouds will fade, the path of new opportunities, goals, and dreams will
blossom. Triumph blossoms when hard trials and tribulations transform
into strength and wisdom. The clouded glasses of fear and despair fade into
perseverance and determination when we embrace our purpose and destiny.

Change transforms, balances, renews, and brings a new level of self-
discovery, peace, love, and joy. Moving to the next level in God opens
opportunities to bless others. Many are lost in a sea of crowds, smiling with
hidden tears and sleepless nights.

There is a level beyond the pain, where the smiles are real, the laughter is loud, the love is deep, and the friendship is real. Don't give up; you're almost there. Your divine destiny leads to freedom, peace, and purpose.

"If the Son therefore shall make you free,
ye shall be free indeed."
(John 8:36, KJV)

DELIVERANCE

God heals when we hurt, enriches our lives through lessons learned, and strengthens us through the growth process. God is always working behind the scenes with our future in mind. We can place our trust in God, knowing He will bring deliverance and restoration in times of opposition and adversity. God strengthens hearts, encourages minds, rejuvenates bodies, enriches souls, and gives us a positive spirit.

"Call upon me in the day of trouble:
I will deliver thee, and thou shalt glorify me."
(Psalm 50:15, KJV)

ENJOY THE JOURNEY

Each day gives us the opportunity to create memories. Family and friends are priceless jewels. Enjoy the journey, as God develops and prepares you for the next level. Enter the future with a thankful mind, a grateful heart, and a positive spirit.

"In all thy ways acknowledge him, and he shall direct thy paths."
(Proverbs 3:6, KJV)

TRIUMPH

Triumph follows perseverance; overcoming adversity places us in position to embrace our purpose and destiny. We become stronger and wiser, and living testimonies of God's love, grace, provision, and mercy. Be ready— your time is now!

"Now thanks be unto God, which always causeth us to triumph in Christ."
(2 Corinthians 2:14, KJV)

OPTIMISM

Don't let circumstances define who you are; they are stepping-stones to triumph and victory. Optimism is a personal choice; each day is an opportunity to pursue your dreams. You have so much to offer the world; people are waiting to be blessed by your talent and expertise. Don't give up; keep moving forward in God's divine plan for your life.

> *"And let us not be weary in well doing:*
> *for in due season we shall reap, it we faint not."*
> *(Galatians 6:9, KJV)*

ENJOY LIFE—IT'S PRICELESS

Sometimes we forsake the present by focusing on the future. Feel the strength of today by not taking your health, family, and friends for granted. Salute the present in all its glory, lessons, and growth opportunities. Enjoy and appreciate life—it's a priceless treasure.

> *"Rejoice in the Lord always: and again, I say, Rejoice."*
> *(Philippians 4:4, KJV)*

ARISE

Transform fear with courage, doubt with hope, negativity with a positive spirit. Despite what you're going through today, you are not alone. God is waiting for you to arise in faith, knowing your strength lies in Him.

> *"With God all things are possible."*
> *(Matthew 19:26, KJV)*

> ***Family and friends are priceless jewels.***

FRIENDSHIP

Let's honor great friendships today! Despite busy schedules, friends always find a way to connect on a special level. No matter what comes, or the size of our circles, good friends are priceless jewels. Take the time to appreciate a friend today.

F - Friends are the jewels of a lifetime.

R - Real friends enjoy seeing God's best in you.

I - I will be the friend others cherish.

E - Everyone needs a friend during life's journey.

N - Now is the time to appreciate the friends who strengthen you.

D - Don't ever underestimate the power of true friendship.

It's not the quantity, but the quality of true friendships that change the world. Friends are priceless jewels. They enhance our vision and encourage, uplift, and bring out the very best in us. God shows His love through treasured friendships that are more like family. So, let's treasure our friendships today, one at a time.

"There is a friend that sticketh closer than a brother."
(Proverbs 18:24, KJV)

CELEBRATING FRIENDSHIP

Friendship is a priceless gift from God. We are blessed to be surrounded by those who bring out the best in us, encouraging us to fulfill our dreams, helping us to reach the place God has destined for us. Friendship transcends the boundaries of blood, and is brought together by matters of the heart and deep concern for one's well-being. Friends are God's way of smiling at us.

"A friend loveth at all times, and a brother is born for adversity."
(Proverbs 17:17, KJV)

FRIENDSHIP IS CHOSEN

People in our lives add so much to the content of our character. Friends that speak hope, strength, joy, and truth are gifts from God. Friendship is chosen and earned through exchanges of trust; it's a special gift from God to help us through life's journey. Have you told your friends how grateful you are for them? If not, pause and do it today!

"Iron sharpeneth iron; so a man sharpeneth the countenance of his friend."
(Proverbs 27:17, KJV)

Action Items:

1. Tell your friends and family how much you love and appreciate them.
2. Name three things that make you a good friend.
3. What steps will you take to "enjoy your journey"?

CHAPTER 8

℮

Encouragement Is a Gift

Your encouragement can make a positive difference in someone's life.

CELEBRATING OTHERS
A positive spirit celebrates the strength, integrity, character, and grace in others. There is wisdom, honor, and joy in building others up rather than tearing them down. We embrace, uplift, encourage, and appreciate the talent in others, knowing we are uniquely and beautifully made. We can embrace and uplift others regardless of color, creed, religion, or ideology.

> *"We give thanks to God always for you all,*
> *making mention of you in our prayers."*
> *(1 Thessalonians 1:2, KJV)*

HEALING
Physical, spiritual, and emotional healing require faith, believing deliverance is available. Healing doesn't always happen the way we expect, and it catches us by surprise. May God grant deliverance in the lives of the brokenhearted, destitute, sick, and afflicted, and those without hope.

We declare victory for positive change, burdens to be lifted, bodies to be healed, and for God to uplift the hearts of those feeling overwhelmed by adversity and opposition.

We pray God will open doors, grant opportunities, and send divine healing to those in need. May better days unfold, futures shine brighter, and days ahead be filled with God's divine favor, purpose, and healing in our lives. Amen.

> *"Beloved, I wish above all things that thou mayest prosper and be in health,*
> *even as thy soul prospereth."*
> *(3 John 1:2, KJV)*

HEALING POWER

Whatever your need is today, trust that God is working with your future in mind. He is ready and available to meet your needs. There is no burden too heavy, situation too hard, or mountain too high for God to reach you right where you are. Regardless of what your need is today, trust God to work it out on your behalf.

"Ask, and ye shall receive, that your joy may be full."
(John 16:24, KJV)

TRIUMPH

Whatever your situation is today, God is ready to meet your needs. Don't give up during the storm, because sunshine is just a few steps away. Be of good courage; you are not alone. There are those who've come out of similar situations victoriously. Despite what it seems like right now, triumph is on its way!

"But they that wait upon the Lord shall renew their strength;
they shall mount up with wings as eagles;
they shall run, and not be weary; and they shall walk, and not faint."
(Isaiah 40:31, KJV)

There is so much beauty inside of you.

YOU ARE SPECIAL

Despite what's going on in your life, you are special. Overcoming obstacles gives strength and preparation for our next level in God. We are extraordinary, destined to be living testimonies of God's love, grace, and mercy. Be encouraged and persevere with faith, knowing God is always working with your future in mind.

"I can do all things through Christ which strengtheneth me."
(Philippians 4:13, KJV)

Reach for your blessings.

LOOK UP

When the weight of the world is on your shoulders, look up and see God's grace. When it seems like everything is going wrong, and your current situation seems insurmountable, look up and see God's mercy. When it seems like your problems are greater than your blessings, look up and see God's strength. When you feel like you're alone in the middle of adversity, look up, knowing God is there, waiting for you to look up and trust Him.

"Ask, and it shall be given you; seek, and ye shall find; knock,
and it shall be opened unto you."
(Matthew 7:7, KJV)

Be the vessel for positivity in the world.

SMILE

A smile can brighten the darkest room. When we smile, we choose victory over our circumstances, knowing God has a divine purpose for our lives. Let's change the world one smile at a time. The smallest gesture can have a profound impact in someone's life. Be the vessel for positivity in the world.

"Rejoicing in hope; patient in tribulation; continuing instant in prayer."
(Romans 12:12, KJV)

KINDNESS

Kindness can make a positive difference in someone's life. We can transform lives through our positive interactions with others. Let's be living examples of God's love through our lives with a positive spirit. Kindness is a priceless gesture. Together, we can use it to change the world!

"She openeth her mouth with wisdom;
and in her tongue is the law of kindness."
(Proverbs 31:26, KJV)

Action Items:
1. What will you do differently as a result of reading this book?
2. How can you be a positive spirit?
3. What unique gift has God placed within you to share with the world?

*"You are a beautiful being, full of life
and wonderful talent to offer the world."*
-A Positive Spirit

Epilogue

God wants to be first in your life, knowing His way is always better than our own. His best work is done when we give Him the driver's seat and let go of the wheel. Relax, sit in the passenger seat, and listen to His voice as He directs your path.

Sometimes it's hard to understand why bad things happen to good people. Life's journey brings us to a place of seasonal blessings. There are times in our lives where pain, hurt, and misery bring anxiety and depression. God is right there, ready to meet your needs right where you are. You are not alone; let Him be your strength during life's storms.

Postscript

Website
www.APositiveSpirit.com

Facebook Page
www.Facebook.com/Encouragement123

Instagram
Sheila_godfrey_edwards

Twitter
@edwardssheila

Blog
Sheilagodfreyedwards.blogspot.com

Email
edwardssheila@frontier.com

Bibliography

The Bible – King James Version
Old and New Testaments

About the Author

Sheila Edwards is a motivational leadership consultant and the CEO of A Positive Spirit, LLC, with a vision to uplift the world through positivity by sharing God's love, mercy, and grace. She is a vision-driven, goal-focused leader, with a proven history of innovation and achievement. Sheila enjoys harnessing team strengths to improve organizational performance.

Throughout her thirty-year career, she has established a reputation as a transformational leader who is driven by challenge, undeterred by obstacles, and committed to furthering standards of excellence. Her ability to build consensus among corporate teams and stakeholders to promote transparency and influence change has been repeatedly proven.

Sheila is a leadership consultant and motivational speaker for corporate, non-profit, political, state, religious, and volunteer organizations. She is a champion for diversity and inclusion and received a five-star review for her 2019 "Diversity & Inclusion" speech at the Mayor's Community & Volunteer Appreciation Open House.

She is a living example of achieving success despite hindering circumstances. She grew up in the housing projects of San Francisco, graduated from Lowell High School, and was the first in her immediate family to graduate from a four-year college and own a home. She graduated from San Francisco State University with a Bachelor of Arts degree in speech communication, with a minor in social science. Sheila has over thirty years of leadership experience and has reached over thirty-eight countries with her ministry and leadership through A Positive Spirit.

Sheila grew up in the church and has served in many leadership roles. She served as both the state Sunday school field representative and state Purity Class president for Greater Northern California Second Jurisdiction. Sheila also served as the state education coordinator for Greater Northern California First Jurisdiction. She enjoyed being a licensed evangelist missionary for many years and working in leadership roles for the Greater San Francisco District. She served as the District Young People's Willing Workers (YPWW) chairlady for many years. Many of her former students serve in leadership capacities throughout the world. It is her divine destiny to give back to the world through the ministry of sharing God's love, mercy, and grace.

The world is suffering in silence, with many secretly contemplating the meaning of life and feeling betrayed by life's circumstances. If we reach up and see God, knowing He has not forgotten about us, His grace, love, and mercy will sustain and protect us throughout life's journey. Sheila's vision is to be a liaison for ministry, medical organizations, and foundations, to support mental health awareness. Together we can change the world by sharing our testimonies of overcoming opposition and living victoriously in God.

CPSIA information can be obtained
at www.ICGtesting.com
Printed in the USA
BVHW031118250822
645505BV00013B/851